D0555488

Schoolies™

Time for Recess

Based on the characters created by
Ellen Crimi-Trent

priddy books

For cousins Sid and Suzy Snail,
recess was always the same.

Out in the playground,
Sid sat under the tree
with his book.

He noticed Suzy playing on her skateboard with her friends. It looked like fun! Just for today, he didn't feel like reading.

Suzy rolled around on her skateboard,
but she felt tired and wasn't having any fun.

Suzy saw Sid reading his book. Just for today, she felt like sitting still.

Suzy rolled over to where Sid sat.
She looked at Sid's book.

Sid looked at Suzy's skateboard.

Suzy sighed. She wanted to be quiet and read a good book.

Sid sighed. He wanted to shout and
play with the other Schoolies.

All at once, Suzy and Sid
made up their minds
to try something new.

May I read
your book,
Sid?

Quietly, Sid rolled over to where Spencer was roller skating. He felt nervous.

Hi!

But Spencer hadn't noticed Sid.
He was having too much fun!

Sid looked back at his favorite
tree and his favorite book.
He was unsure what to do.

Then Spencer saw Sid, and soon enough,
Sid was having lots of fun rolling around, too.

Under the tree, Suzy watched Sid for a while.
She wondered if the Schoolies missed her.

Then she opened up the book
and started to read.

Suzy could hear the sounds of the Schoolies playing, but soon she was lost in her story.

Too soon, the bell rang for the end of recess. **Brrring! Brrring!**

Suzy and Sid went back inside to their classroom.

Here's your skateboard, Suzy.

Here's your book, Sid.

Just for today, it was fun
to try something new.

Maybe they'd try something
new again tomorrow.